Easy words to read

Hen's pens

Phil Roxbee Cox

Illustrated by Stephen Cartwright

Edited by Jenny Tyler

Language consultant:

Marlynne Grant

BSc, CertEd, MEdPsych, PhD, AFBPs, CPsychol

There is a yellow duck to find on every page.

First published in 2001 by Usborne Publishing Ltd. Usborne House, 83-85 Saffron Hill, London EC1N 8RT, England. www.usborne.com

Copyright © 2001 Usborne Publishing Ltd.

Hen has new pens.

She has ten
new pens.

3

"When will you use your new pens, Hen?"

"Now, Brown Cow!"

"What will you draw?"

"Straw...

5

... and the big blue sky,
and a yellow bird flying by."

"And zigzags are better than ALL the rest."

Hen hops off her nest.

"Drawing patterns is
what I like best."

She zigs and zags from left to right.

... until her paper
has run out.

She zigs and zags all day and night...

"What can I draw on now?" she shouts.

"Draw on your eggs!" says Brown Cow.

"Draw big dots on your eggs."
"Or more zigzags?" Hen begs.

Hen's zigzags are very bright indeed.

"Zigzags are just what ALL eggs need!"

...if I zigzag
all the eggs
I find."

"I'm sure the others will not mind...

Now everyone's eggs are in a dreadful mix.

Sorting them out
is hard to fix.

Hen has made a bad mistake.
That's not her chick.

It's a baby snake!